P.E. Nikolajsen

Domino-Knitted
Shawls

Akacia

Domino-Knitted Shawls
By Poul Erik Nikolajsen
Design, layout and photo: Poul Erik Nikolajsen
Translated by Lone Dalgaard from Sjaler i dominostrik.

© 2013 Forlaget Akacia
Skovvænget 1
5690 Tommerup
Denmark
www.akacia.dk

Printed at InPrint, Riga, 2013

ISBN: 978-87-7847-121-5

Preface

The background for this book is actually rather sad as I was not the one to write it - it was my sister, Inge Lise.

For many years, Inge Lise was the editor of Danish Needlework Magazine published by my publishing house, but as her health began to fail, and we had to stop the production of the magazine, she and a friend decided to write a book on shawls. Unfortunately, nothing ever came of the project.

Among the papers she had left behind, I later found a page with little sketches of shawls, 23 in all to be precise, of many different shapes and with very different patterns.

I thought about this for a while and toyed with the idea that it could be fun to find out how all those ideas could be used if they were to be combined with the domino knitting technique.

To begin with, this gave rise to quite a lot of thought. For how could a round shawl be combined with domino knitting, which in its nature consists only of squares? Well, to draw the shawls was easy but would it also be possible to knit them?

Fortunately, I know some very skilled knitters who were really challenged by converting my ideas into something tangible, and I owe a lot to Ruth, Annelise, Hanne and Anny for the great work they performed.

I hope that others will have as much fun knitting the shawls as I had designing them.

Enjoy!

Poul Erik Nikolajsen

Contents

Shawl 1 – p. 14
Intermediate

Shawl 2 – p. 18
Advanced

Shawl 3 – p. 24
Advanced

Shawl 4 – p. 28
Advanced

Shawl 5 – p. 32
Beginner

Shawl 6 – p. 36
Beginner

Shawl 7 – p. 40
Intermediate

Shawl 8 – p. 44
Intermediate

Shawl 9 – p. 48
Advanced

Shawl 10 – p. 52
Advanced

Shawl 11 – p. 56
Advanced

Shawl 12 – p. 60
Intermediate

Shawl 13 – p. 64
Advanced

Shawl 14 – p. 68
Intermediate

Shawl 15 – p. 72
Intermediate

Shawl 16 – p. 76
Intermediate

How to Knit a Domino Square

In domino knitting, you will always need an uneven number of stitches: 1 centre stitch and x stitches on either side of it. The idea is to knit 2 stitches together around the centre stitch to create a square. That is the groundwork of domino knitting.

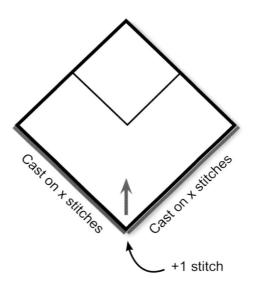

The blue arrow shows the knitting direction of the square.

Cast on 2 times x stitches + 1 stitch (= an uneven number).

1st row (wrong side): Work to the last stitch, purl 1.
On all the following wrong side rows: Slip 1, work to the last stitch, purl 1. Mark the centre stitch with a marker or a thread.

2nd row (right side): Slip 1 and work to the stitch before the centre stitch. The decrease at the centre can be made in two different ways (see 'How to Decrease at the Centre', page 7). Work to the last stitch, purl 1.
There are now 2 stitches less in the row.

3rd row (wrong side): Slip 1, knit to the last stitch, purl 1.

4th row (right side): Work as the 2nd row.

5th row (wrong side): Work as the 3rd row.

ETC.

Continue decreasing twice at the middle of the right side row. Note that every decrease will reduce the number of stitches by 2, 1 stitch at each side of the centre stitch. When there are 3 stitches left on the right side row, knit a double decrease. The square is now finished.

How to Decrease at the Centre

The double decrease at the centre can be worked in two different ways. There will always be 2 stitches less in the row, no matter which method you use.

Ordinary decrease
Slip 1, knit 2 together and pass the slipped stitch over.

Decrease with distinct knit stitches
Slip 2 together, knit 1 and pass the 2 slipped stitches over.
Purl the stitch on the wrong side.

How to Add More Squares

One square is not enough for a shawl, so more are needed.

Add a square to the left
Note that the stitch forming the new centre stitch has to be cast on.

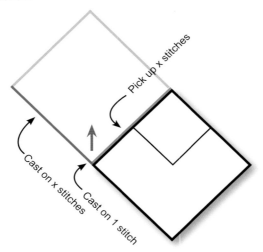

Add a square to the right
Note that the stitch forming the new centre stitch has to be cast on.

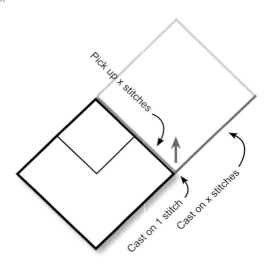

Add a square between two squares

In this case, the centre stitch must be cast on between the two sides. If there is a square immediately under the new one, the centre stitch must be picked up in the top of that square. By doing so you avoid holes between the squares, and it will be easier to get the centre stitch running as a continuous highlight across several squares.

How to Pick up Stitches

Join the domino squares neatly by picking up stitches in the front loop of the edge stitch only.

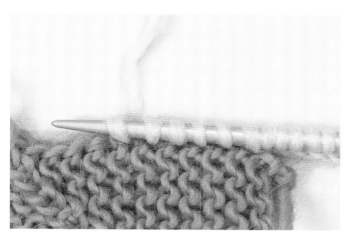

Right side.

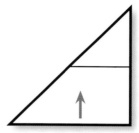

Wrong side: Note that stitches have only been picked up in the front loop of the edge stitch.

Incomplete Squares

In order to get the right edge on the shawls, you will often need half a square.

Right half of a domino square

1st row (wrong side):
Knit to the last stitch, purl 1.
On all the following wrong side rows: Slip 1, knit to the last stitch, purl 1.

2nd row (right side):
Slip 1. Knit until there are 3 stitches left. Knit 2 together and purl the last stitch.

Left half of a domino square

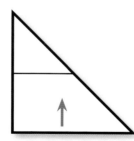

1st row (wrong side):
Purl 1, knit the remaining stitches.

2nd row (right side):
Slip 1 knit wise, knit 2 together, knit, purl the last stitch.

'Inverted square'

In some of the patterns, you will need a square that is worked from the outside in towards the centre.

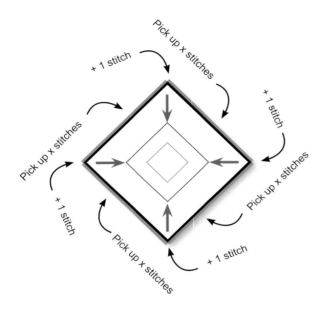

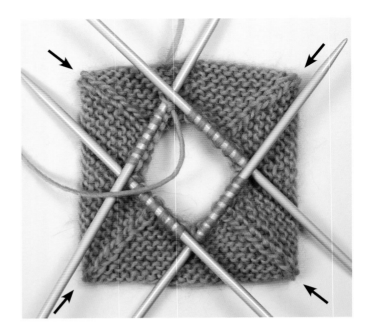

Pick up, or cast on, x stitches on all sides: the same number of stitches on each of the four sides + 4 corner stitches. The same applies here as for ordinary squares: If possible, the corner stitches should be picked up in the adjacent centre stitch.

This square is knitted as if it were four separate squares.

If you have to work with a large number of stitches, begin with circular needles. Continue with double pointed needles when the number of stitches has been reduced. And a tip: You will get the best result if the needles are placed so that the 'corners' are positioned at the middle of the needles and not in the corners - see the illustration on the right.

Bottom half of a domino square

To get a straight upper edge, the empty spaces between two domino squares must be filled in.

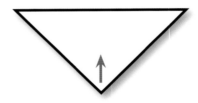

1st row (wrong side): Slip 1 purl wise with the yarn in front of the work. Work to the last stitch and purl 1.

2nd row (right side): Slip 1 knit wise, knit 2 together through the back loops, work x, 'centre stitch', work x, knit 2 together, purl 1 (= 4 stitches less).

The following wrong side row: Slip 1, work to the last stitch and purl 1.

The following right side row: Slip 1 knit wise, knit 2 together through the back loops, work x, 'centre stitch', work x, knit 2 together, purl 1 (= I4 stitches less).

Last row: 'centre stitch' (= 1 stitch).

Pull the stitch long, cut the yarn and pull the end through the long stitch. Pull it slightly

Square without a top point

In one of the patterns (Shawl no. 16), a square without a top point is used. Begin with an ordinary domino square, but cast off in the usual way after a number of garter ridges.

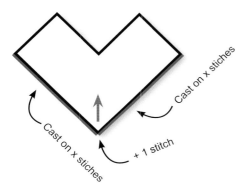

Elongated square

In several of the patterns, elongated squares are used. This may sound strange, but the idea is quite simple - normally, decreases are made at the centre of a square, but in this case you also have to increase.
Each time a stitch is decreased at the centre, an increase of 1 stitch should be made at the edge, and the result is that you work straight up.

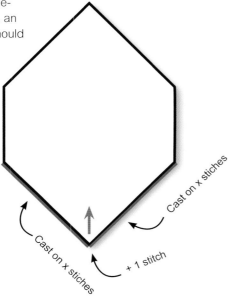

Square with one side missing

To get a straight edge on the shawl, it is often necessary to cut off one side of a domino square.
This is typically done by removing half of the stitches at one side.
At the side with half the number of stitches, increase 1 stitch at the edge - just like in the 'elongated square' - at the same time as you decrease at the centre. When half of the number of garter ridges are worked, you stop increasing.
The side with the full number of stitches is worked as a normal domino square.

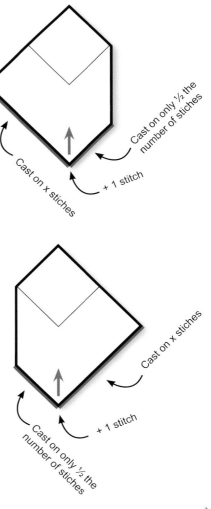

More Techniques

Fasten off as you knit

The best way to fasten off ends is to do it as you go along - and so avoid having to do it afterwards with a needle. When you fasten off as much as possible in this way, it will no longer be a problem to work with many colours. It is difficult to fasten off in this way on the wrong side, so try to avoid doing that. Ends at the left edge are fastened off as you come across them, or later with a needle. Always fasten off the lower end first. When it has been fastened off, you can fasten off the end that is NOW the lower one, etc.

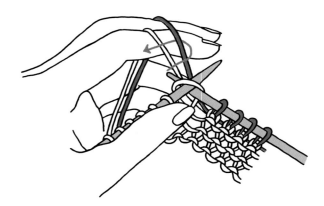

Do not cut off the ends right away, but work a couple of rows after they have been fastened off and cut them off about 1 cm from the work. If you cut off ends too closely to the work, they can easily slip through to the right side of the work in the wash.

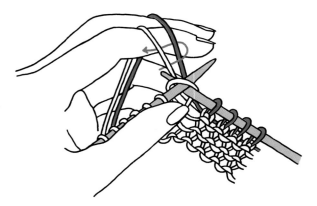

Hold the work with the threads across your fingers. Place the colour that you will work with (the 'new' colour) closest to your fingertips (red on the sketch) across 2 fingers (index and middle finger) and the 'old' colour closest to your hand (light colour on the sketch) across one finger (index finger). So 'new' is the yarn you will work with next and 'old' is the end to be fastened off.

Place the needle under 'old' and work the next stitch with 'new'. Now place the needle over 'old' and work the next stitch with 'new'.

Repeat from * to * a couple of times.

Knit cast on

Cast on 1 stitch. Place the needle with the stitch in your left hand and hold the other needle in your right hand.
Work the stitch [Figure 1]. Let the first stitch stay on the left hand needle and slip the new stitch twisted onto the needle next to the first stitch on the left hand needle [Figure 2]. There are now 2 stitches on the needle. Work 1 in the new stitch in the same way and slip it onto the needle to the other 2 stitches (= 3 stitches). Continue in this way until you have the required number of stitches.

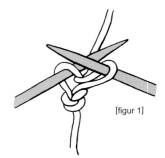

[figur 1]

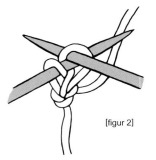

[figur 2]

Garter ridges

1 garter ridge = 2 knit rows.

These 2 rows make a ridge and are only referred to as ridges in the patterns.
In the patterns ridges are counted.

How to join squares

Begin at the bottom, knit up 1 stitch on the right side in the first cast on stitch at the right side – note: knit up stitches through <u>both</u> loops.

Then work x stitches, 1 stitch in each edge stitch through <u>both</u> loops and knit 1 in the last stitch.

How to Read the Patterns

The sketches depicted in the patterns show numbers and letters in the order in which to work the individual squares.

2-2-2-2-2-6

16 sts   16 sts

1 st

In addition, the individual elements of the pattern are shown. The numbers next to the elements show how many stitches should be cast on/picked up along the edge.
The row of numbers above the elements shows how many ridges to work in each colour. So in this example, there are 5 stripes of 2 ridges each and 6 ridges in the last colour at the end.

In some cases, this is written in a different way, such as '2 ridges in each colour'. The meaning is the same, but here there are of course not 6 ridges at the end.

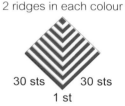

2 ridges in each colour

30 sts   30 sts

1 st

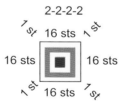

2-2-2-2

1 st   16 sts   1 st

16 sts   16 sts

1 st   16 sts   1 st

In the same way, the numbers surrounding an 'inverted square' show how many stitches should be cast on/picked up at the edge. There also, the numbers above the square also here show how many ridges there are in each stripe.

In a few patterns, there are shapes like this one with abbreviations such as 28r. The abbreviation shows that there should be 28 ridges up along the left side of the finished shape.

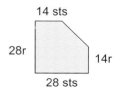

14 sts

28r   14r

28 sts

Shawl no 1

It is easy to get shawls of this shape to stay on your shoulders.

Intermediate

ROWAN
Pure Wool DK
Enamel - 013

6 balls

ROWAN
Pure Wool DK
Damson - 030

2 balls

ROWAN
Pure Wool DK
Hyacinth - 026

4 balls

Techniques
Knit cast on
Garter stitch
All squares are worked with decreases with distinct knit stitches

Description
Work the two side panels in the order
A - B - C.
Gather the two panels with a stripe of 'inverted squares'.

10cm/4in
10cm/4in — 30 rows
22 sts

UK
8
US
6
4 mm

Finished size:
App. 144 x 72 cm

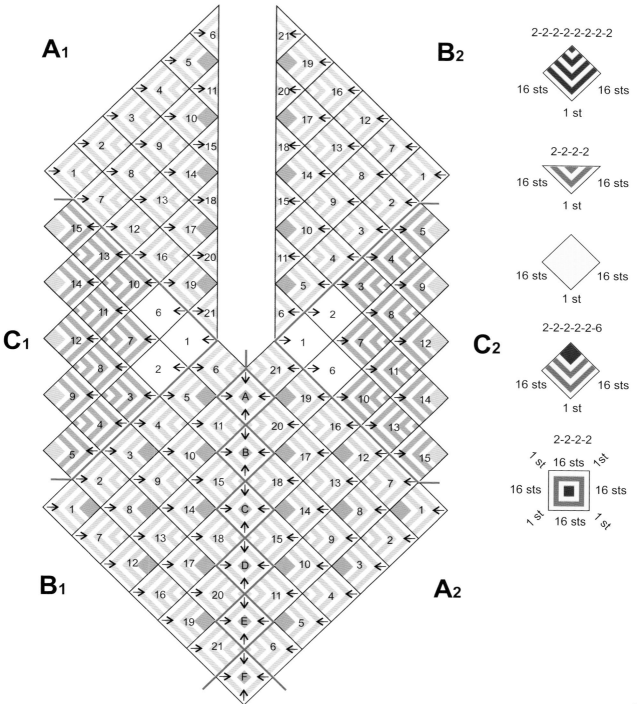

A₁

B₂

2-2-2-2-2-2-2-2
16 sts   16 sts
1 st

2-2-2-2
16 sts   16 sts
1 st

16 sts   16 sts
1 st

C₁

C₂

2-2-2-2-2-6
16 sts   16 sts
1 st

B₁

A₂

2-2-2-2
1 st   16 sts   1 st
16 sts   16 sts
1 st   16 sts   1 st

17

Shawl no 2

This model is inspired by the Faroese shawl which is characterized by its "build-in" shoulders giving it a unique fit.
As the tips of this shawl are turning forward, it has some of the same effect. It is easier to get the shawl to stay on your shoulders than if the upper edge was completely straight.

Advanced

ROWAN
Pure Wool DK
Enamel - 013

5 balls

ROWAN
Pure Wool DK
Pier - 006

3 balls

ROWAN
Pure Wool DK
Raspberry - 028

2 balls

ROWAN
Pure Wool DK
Port - 037

5 balls

Techniques
Knit cast on
Garter stitch
All squares are worked with ordinary decreases

Description
See page 23

1 ridge in each colour

22 sts   22 sts
1 st

1 ridge in each colour

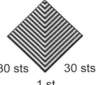

30 sts   30 sts
1 st

22 sts   22 sts
1 st

1-1-1-1-1-1-1-1-7

15 sts   15 sts
1 st

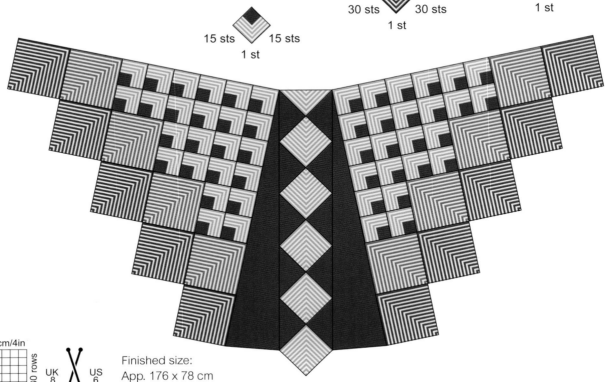

10cm/4in
10cm/4in
30 rows
22 sts

UK 8   US 6
4 mm

Finished size:
App. 176 x 78 cm

20

ROWAN
Pure Wool DK
Enamel - 013

5 balls

ROWAN
Pure Wool DK
Marine - 008

5 balls

Techniques
Knit cast on
Garter stitch
All squares are worked with decreases with
distinct knit stitches

ROWAN
Pure Wool DK
Pier - 006

4 balls

2 ridges in each colour

30 sts   30 sts
1 st

2 ridges in each colour

22 sts   22 sts
1 st

22 sts   22 sts
1 st

1-1-1-1-1-1-1-1-7

15 sts   15 sts
1 st

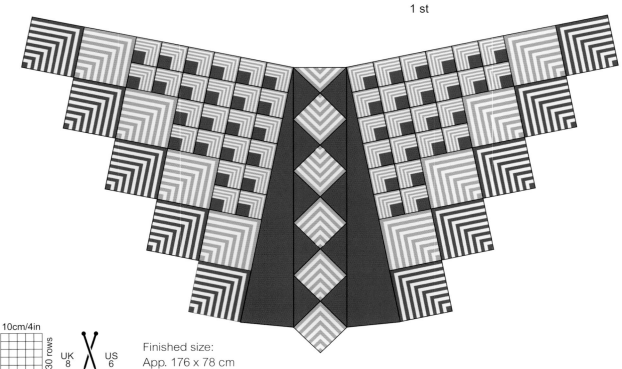

10cm/4in

10cm/4in   30 rows

22 sts

UK 8   US 6

4 mm

Finished size:
App. 176 x 78 cm

Description

Begin with the back parts A 1 – 6.

Continue with A 7 – 16.
Begin the triangles at the bottom.
Pick up 2 stitches, turn, knit 2, pick up 1 stitch purl wise.
Turn, knit 3, and pick up 1 stitch knit wise. Turn, knit 2, knit 2 together, and pick up 1 stitch purl wise. Turn, knit 4, and pick up 1 stitch knit wise. Turn, knit 5, and pick up 1 stitch purl wise. Turn, knit 4, knit 2 together, and pick up 1 stitch knit wise. Continue in this way and knit 2 together on each 3rd row until all stitches at the edges at both sides have been picked up.

On B2, work 1 row before beginning the shortened rows.

B1 and B2.
Knit the next 7 stitches, turn and work back, turn 7 stitches before on the next row, work back. Turn 4,7,5,10,6,6,9,6,9,6,9,8,6, 7,7,7,7,7,7,7 stitches before the last turn. On the 15th and 29th rows: knit 2 together at the beginning of the row on B1, and at the end of the row on B2.

Work C1 and C2 directly on to B1 and B2.

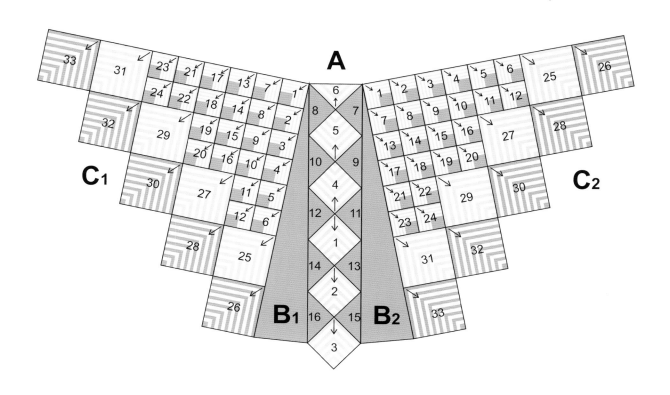

23

Shawl no 3

This shawl begins one third in and is worked from the outside in. Finish with a border all around.

The reason why this shawl is worked in this way is that domino is characterized by the decreases up along the centre of the individual squares, and to make this possible you have to knit it from the outside and in towards the centre.

Advanced

Schachenmayr
Alpaka
Leinen Meliert 00105

5 balls

Schachenmayr
Alpaka
Trüffel 00010

5 balls

Techniques
Knit cast on
Garter stitch
All squares are worked with decreases with distinct knit stitches

Schachenmayr
Alpaka
Natur 00002

4 balls

Schachenmayr
Alpaka
Kamel 00004

4 balls

10cm/4in
10cm/4in
29 rows
21 sts

UK
8
US
6

4 mm

4 mm

Finished size:
App. 160 x 60 cm

Description
Part A:

1 ridge in each of the colours
Trüffel and Leinen Meliert
Cast on 592 stitches and work 21 ridges as you decrease in
each of the corners = 424 stitches left. Begin at the red arrow,
105 stitches from the corner.
TIP: Due to the large number of stitches on row A, it is a good
idea to place a marker after every 21 stitches.

Part C:

2 ridges in each colour
Kamel and Natur

42 sts   42 sts

1 st

Part B:

1 ridge in each of the colours
Kamel and Natur
Begin each square at the red
arrow, 10 stitches from the
corner.

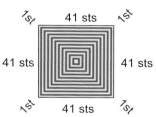

1st   41 sts   1st

41 sts   41 sts

1st   41 sts   1st

Parts D and E:

1 ridge in each of the colours
Light coloured squares:
Kamel and Natur
Dark coloured squares:
Trüffel and Leinen Meliert

21 sts   21 sts

1st

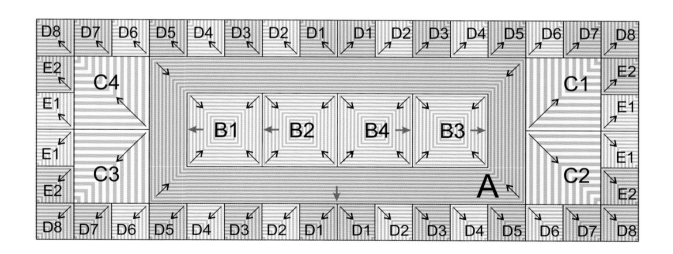

Shawl no 4

Is it possible to mix a round shawl with straight domino squares?
Yes, if you add something in between.
The effect is almost that of a row of fox tales.

Advanced

Schachenmayr
Alpaka
Schwartz 00099

3 balls

Schachenmayr
Alpaka
Kiesel 00095

5 balls

Schachenmayr
Alpaka
Natur 00002

2 balls

Description

Borders:

Work all domino borders first.

Begin the border with the domino square closest to the neckline and continue with a triangle on either side.

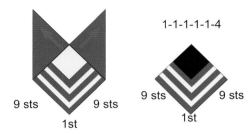

1-1-1-1-1-4

9 sts   9 sts

1st

9 sts   9 sts

1st

Side triangles:

Pick up 9 stitches, decrease at the outer edge on every second row.

Begin the next domino square in the notch between the two triangles.

10cm/4in

10cm/4in   29 rows

21 sts

UK 8   US 6

4 mm

Finished size:
App. 45 cm

Techniques

Knit cast on

Garter stitch

All squares are worked with decreases with distinct knit stitches

Parts A and B:

Parts A and B are worked in the same way. You will, however, need more stitches for Part B. Numbers for Part B are shown in parenthesis.

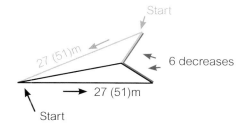

First half:

Pick up 27 (51) stitches.
Decrease 1 stitch on every row.
Work and turn:

1st row: Turn, when there are 6 (11) stitches left.
3rd row: Turn, when there are 11 (21) stitches left.
5th row: Turn, when there are 16 (31) stitches left.
6th row: Work all stitches and slip them onto an extra needle.

Second half (grey on the sketch):

Work as the first half.

Casting off:

Work the stitches on the 2 extra needles together on the wrong side, 1 stitch from each needle, and cast off at the same time.

Part C:

See Joining Squares on page 13. Pick up 1 stitch at the bottom and pick up 1 stitch at either side on all right side rows 7 times = 15 stitches. Cast off.

Part D:

Pick up 120 stitches.
3rd row: Decrease 1 stitch 12 times.
5th row: Decrease 1 stitch 12 times.
Work 12 rows in all. Cast off.

Part E:

Front edges: Pick up about 78 stitches and work 4 rows.
Cast off.

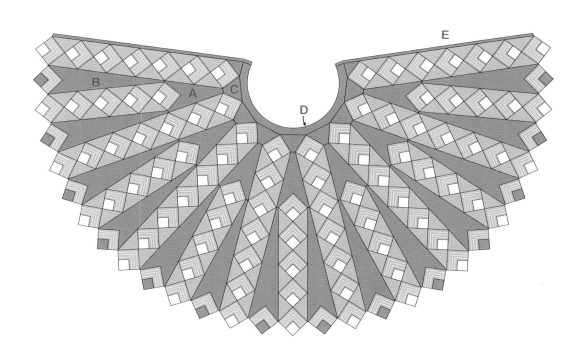

Shawl no 5

It does not always have to be crazy and complicated.
Small, uncomplicated shawl, all in domino.

Beginner

ROWAN

Pure Wool DK
Snow - 012

5 balls

ROWAN

Pure Wool DK
Hyacinth - 026

2 balls

ROWAN

Pure Wool DK
Marine - 008

4 balls

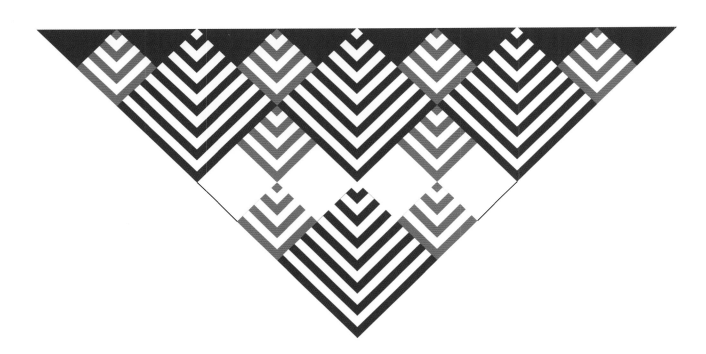

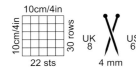

Finished size:
App. 140 x 70 cm

Techniques

Knit cast on
Garter stitch
All squares are worked with decreases with distinct knit stitches

Description

Work the squares in the order shown in the chart.

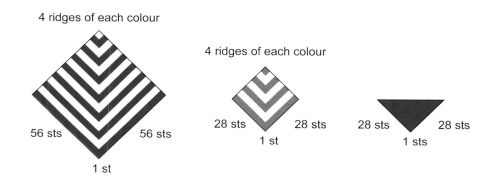

4 ridges of each colour

56 sts   56 sts

1 st

4 ridges of each colour

28 sts   28 sts

1 st

28 sts   28 sts

1 sts

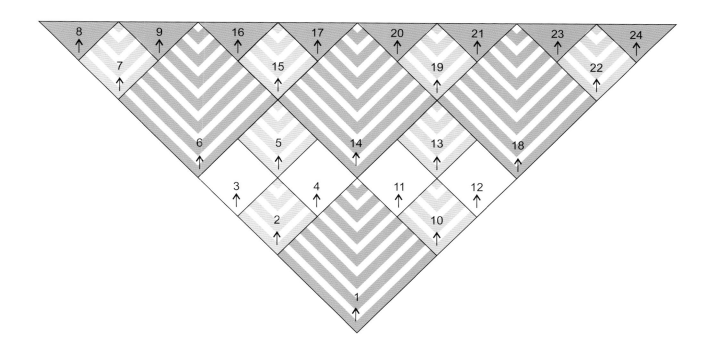

Shawl no 6

This shawl is actually quite simple. The fun is in the way in which it is worked and in the way the stripes are organized. Did anyone mention zebra stripes?

Beginner

ROWAN
Pure Wool DK
Black - 004

7 balls

ROWAN
Pure Wool DK
Hyacinth - 026

2 balls

ROWAN
Pure Wool DK
Snow - 012

8 balls

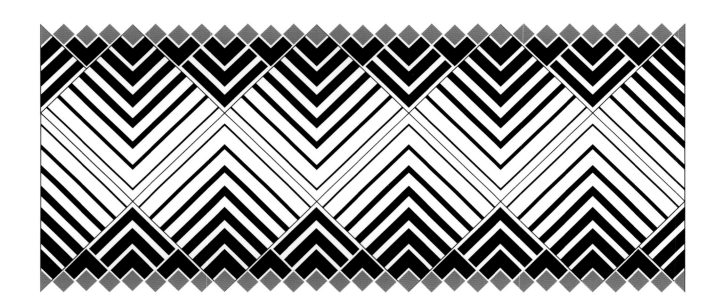

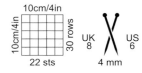

Finished size:
App. 153 x 65 cm

Techniques

Knit cast on

Garter stitch

All squares are worked with decreases with distinct knit stitches

Description

Work the squares in the order shown in the chart.

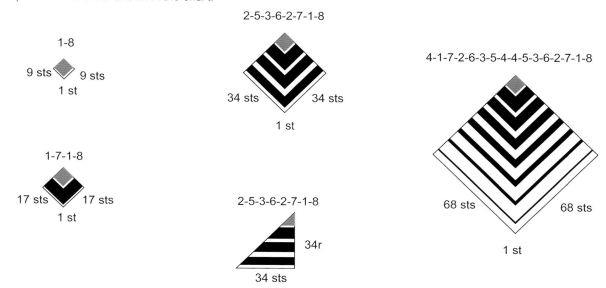

1-8

9 sts ⬦ 9 sts

1 st

2-5-3-6-2-7-1-8

34 sts ◆ 34 sts

1 st

4-1-7-2-6-3-5-4-4-5-3-6-2-7-1-8

68 sts ◆ 68 sts

1 st

1-7-1-8

17 sts ◆ 17 sts

1 st

2-5-3-6-2-7-1-8

34r

34 sts

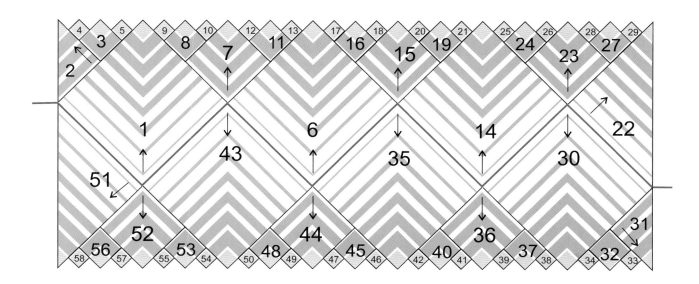

Shawl no 7

Also a rather simple shawl really, but the distinct knit stitches on the four 'inverted squares' on the back renders an interesting effect.

Intermediate

ROWAN
Pure Wool DK
Dahlia - 042

2 balls

ROWAN
Pure Wool DK
Snow - 012

6 balls

ROWAN
Pure Wool DK
Marine - 008

4 balls

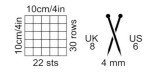

Finished size:
App. 160 x 60 cm

Techniques
Knit cast on
Garter stitch
All blue and red squares are worked with decreases with
distinct knit stitches
All white squares are worked with ordinary decreases

42

Description

Work the squares in the order shown in the chart.

Begin with the centre design and continue with the two blue end pieces.

End with the side panels at the same time joining the first pieces.

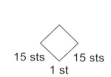

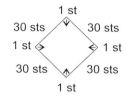

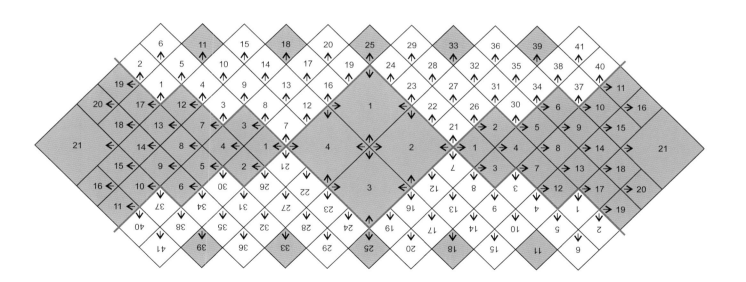

Shawl no 8

There is not much to say about this shawl.
Long narrow shawl with a very spectacular back.

Intermediate

ROWAN
Creative Focus Worsted
Blue Smoke - 03089

2 balls

ROWAN
Creative Focus Worsted
Magenta - 01890

1 balls

ROWAN
Creative Focus Worsted
Natural - 00100

2 balls

ROWAN
Creative Focus Worsted
Lavender Heather - 0712

2 balls

Finished size:
App. 173 x 40 cm

Techniques
Knit cast on
Garter stitch
All squares are worked with decreases with distinct knit stitches

Description

Work the squares in the order shown in the chart.

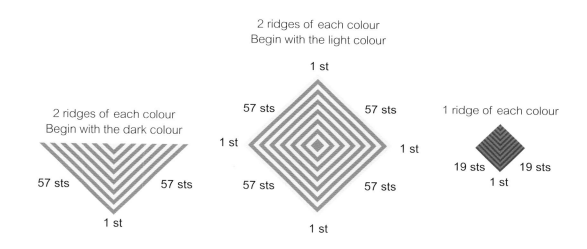

2 ridges of each colour
Begin with the light colour

1 st

57 sts   57 sts

1 st   1 st

57 sts   57 sts

1 st

2 ridges of each colour
Begin with the dark colour

57 sts   57 sts

1 st

1 ridge of each colour

19 sts   19 sts

1 st

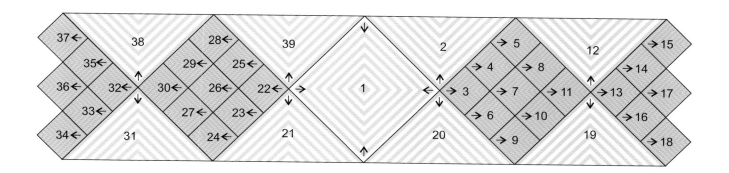

Shawl no 9

It is always a pleasure when one's thoughts and ideas prove so successful.
Begin with the joining stripes and continue with the coloured corners.

Advanced

ROWAN
Creative Focus Worsted
Natural - 00100

5 balls

ROWAN
Creative Focus Worsted
Magenta - 01890

2 balls

ROWAN
Creative Focus Worsted
True Purple - 01800

2 balls

Techniques

Knit cast on
Garter stitch
All squares are worked with decreases with distinct knit stit-ches

Description

Work parts A1-A3, B1-B3, C1-C3 and D1-D3 first, then the coloured corners and end with E, F and G.

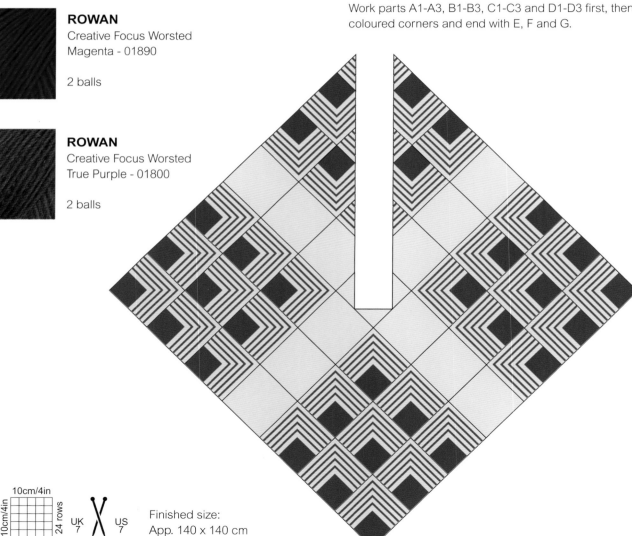

10cm/4in
10cm/4in   24 rows
20 sts

UK
7
US
7
4.5 mm

Finished size:
App. 140 x 140 cm
(from tip to tip)

2-1-2-1-2-1-2-1-2

14r 14 sts   14 sts 14r

2-1-2-1-2-1-2-1-2-14

28 sts   28 sts

1 st

Part A, B, C and D:

28r

28 sts

Part A1:

28 sts

28r   14r

14 sts

Part D1:

14 sts

28r   14r

28 sts

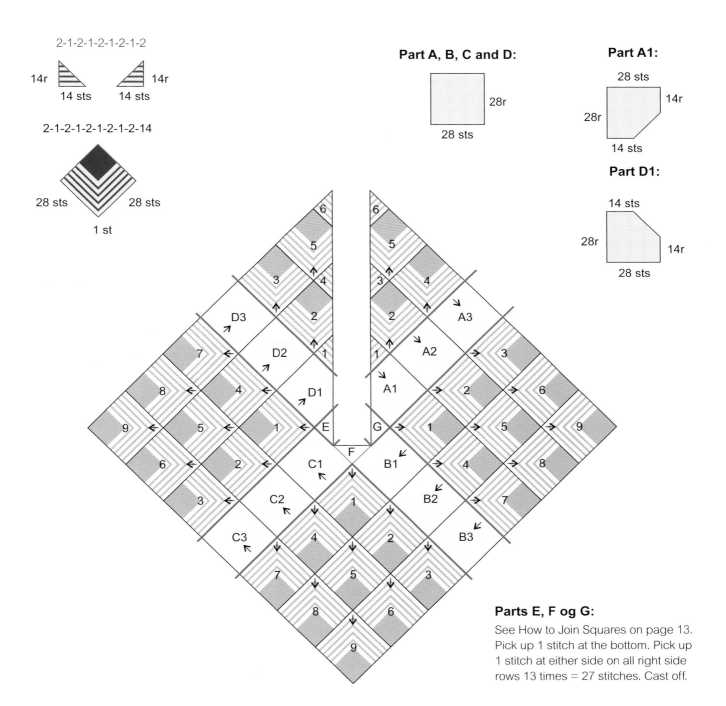

Parts E, F og G:

See How to Join Squares on page 13.
Pick up 1 stitch at the bottom. Pick up
1 stitch at either side on all right side
rows 13 times = 27 stitches. Cast off.

Shawl no 10

The basic design of this shawl in Harlequin colours is the same as of Shawl 9, but to get the white borders it is necessary to work it in the reverse order. On Shawl 9, the joining stripes are worked first and then the coloured corners. On this shawl, the coloured corners are worked first and then joined with the white stripes.

Advanced

ROWAN
Creative Focus Worsted
Natural - 00100

4 balls

ROWAN
Creative Focus Worsted
Saffron - 03810

2 balls

ROWAN
Creative Focus Worsted
Ebony - 00500

2 balls

ROWAN
Creative Focus Worsted
Carmine - 02055

2 balls

ROWAN
Creative Focus Worsted
Delft - 01321

2 balls

Techniques
Knit cast on
Garter stitch
All squares are worked with ordinary decreases

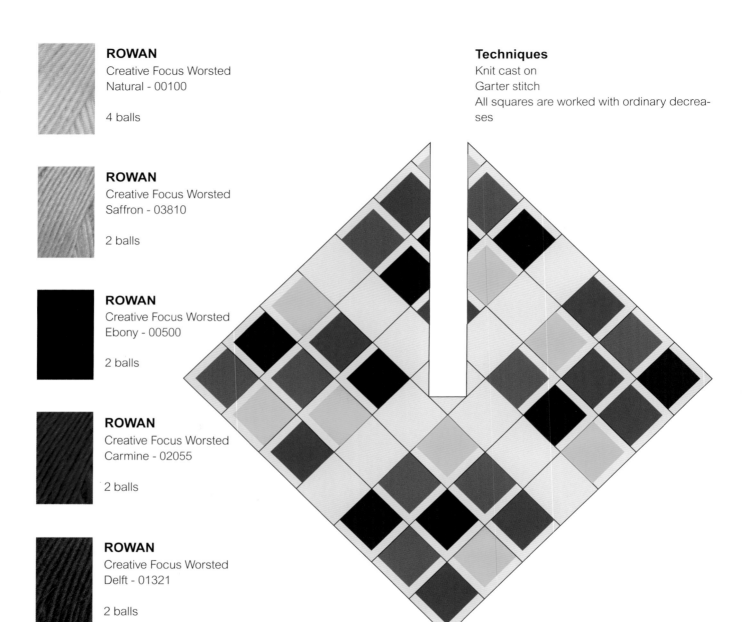

UK
7

US
7

4.5 mm

Finished size:
App. 140x 140 cm
(from tip to tip)

10cm/4in

10cm/4in

24 rows

20 sts

All coloured areas are worked from the same template.

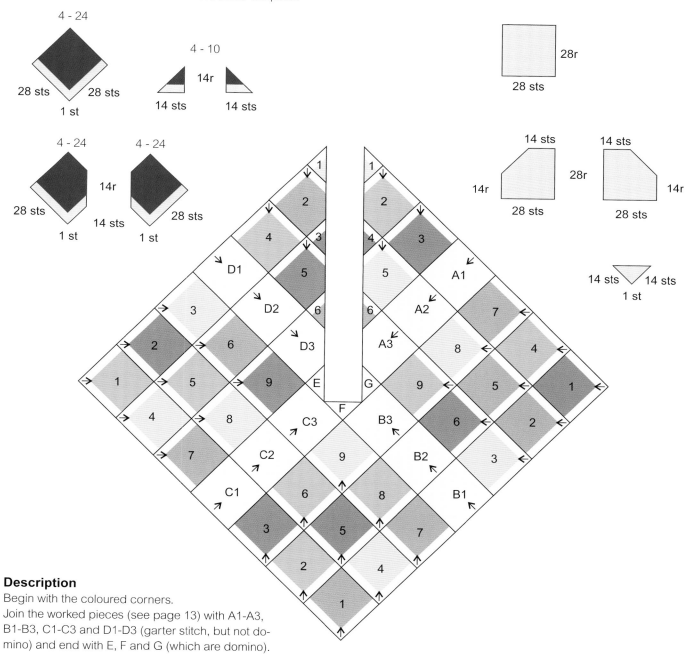

Description

Begin with the coloured corners.
Join the worked pieces (see page 13) with A1-A3, B1-B3, C1-C3 and D1-D3 (garter stitch, but not domino) and end with E, F and G (which are domino).

Shawl no 11

While you work on this shawl, it looks completely hopeless. The order of the individual squares makes it look like one big rag. But just wait until it is finished.

Advanced

ROWAN
Pure Wool DK
Pier - 006

5 balls

ROWAN
Pure Wool DK
Indigo - 010

5 balls

ROWAN
Pure Wool DK
Snow - 012

2 balls

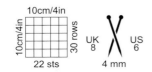

Finished size:
App. 174 x 58 cm

Techniques
Knit cast on
Garter stitch
All squares are worked with decreases with distinct
knit stitches

Description

Work the squares in the order shown in the chart.

Join the parts C-D and E-F (see page 13).

9 - 9

18 sts   18 sts

1st

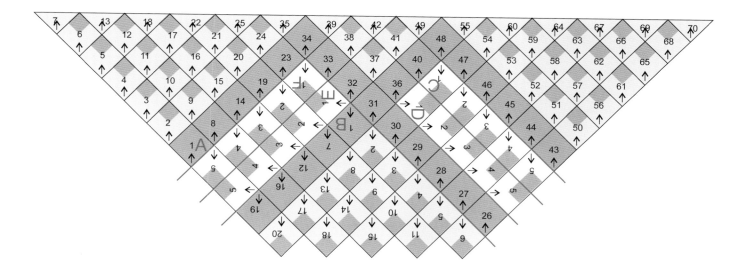

Shawl no 12

Narrow shawl that will stay on your shoulders.
This shawl is rather long, but it can easily be shortened by leaving out the last big square at either end. The border may be worked around the front edge.

Intermediate

ROWAN
Pure Wool DK
Enamel - 013

7 balls

ROWAN
Pure Wool DK
Parsley - 020

1 balls

ROWAN
Pure Wool DK
Black - 004

3 balls

ROWAN
Pure Wool DK
Marine - 008

1 balls

ROWAN
Pure Wool DK
Hyacinth - 026

1 balls

ROWAN
Pure Wool DK
Ox Blood - 049

1 balls

ROWAN
Pure Wool DK
Shale - 002

1 balls

10cm/4in
10cm/4in
30 rows
22 sts
UK 8
US 6
4 mm

Finished size:
App. 174 x 58 cm

Techniques
Knit cast on
Garter stitch
All squares are worked with decreases with distinct knit stitches

Description

Work the squares in the order shown in the chart.

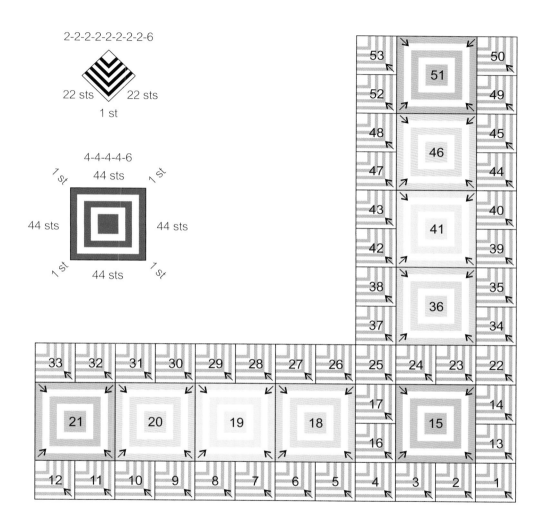

2-2-2-2-2-2-2-2-6

22 sts   22 sts

1 st

4-4-4-4-6

1 st   44 sts   1 st

44 sts   44 sts

1 st   44 sts   1 st

Shawl no 13

In this shawl, all side panels are joined by 'elongated' squares giving it a rather interesting effect on the back.

Advanced

ROWAN
Pure Wool DK
Indigo - 010

3 balls

ROWAN
Pure Wool DK
Port - 037

2 balls

ROWAN
Pure Wool DK
Enamel - 013

5 balls

10cm/4in

10cm/4in

30 rows

22 sts

UK
8

US
6

4 mm

Finished size:
App. 162 x 56 cm

Techniques
Knit cast on
Garter stitch

Description

A-D and I-K are worked with ordinary decreases. E-H are worked with decreases with distinct knit stitches.

First, work parts A-D and then join them with E-H (see page 13).
End with the squares I-L.

(14 ridges of alternating red and white stripes; begin with white, then 14 ridges of white) x 3. 14 ridges of alternating red and white stripes; begin with white and finish with 14 ridges of blue.

14 sts   14 sts

1 st

14 ridges of alternating red and white stripes; begin with red, then 14 ridges of white and 14 ridges of blue.

14 sts   14 sts

1 st

28 sts   28 sts

1 st

28 sts   28 sts

1 st

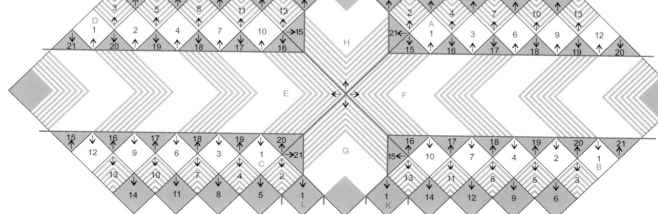

Shawl no 14

The special shape of this shawl almost forms a collar around the neck.

Intermediate

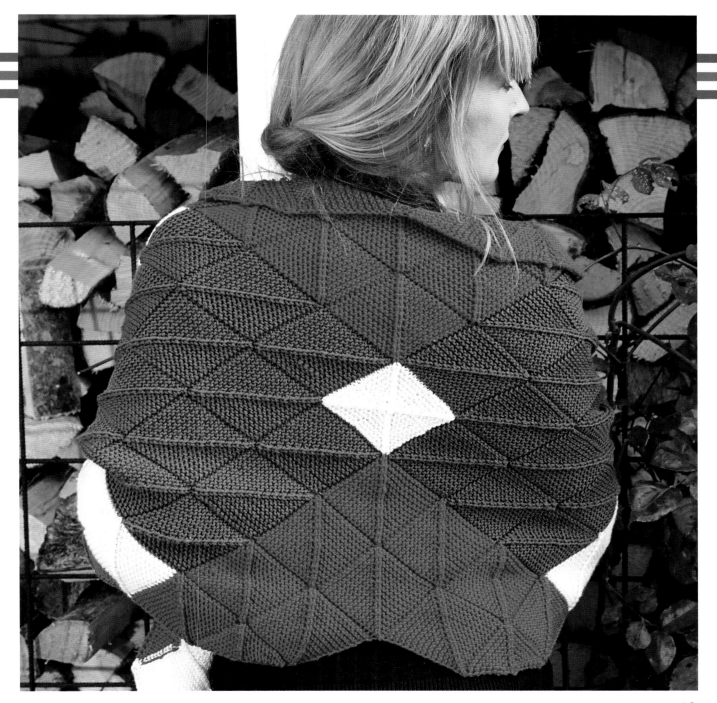

ROWAN
Pure Wool DK
Anthracite - 003

5 balls

ROWAN
Pure Wool DK
Snow - 012

4 balls

Techniques

Knit cast on
Garter stitch
All squares are worked with decreases with distinct
knit stitches

ROWAN
Pure Wool DK
Daliah - 042

3 balls

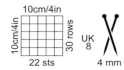

UK
8

US
6

4 mm

Finished size:
App. 160 x 60 cm

Description

Work the squares in the order shown in the chart.

Begin with the two halves (A-B-C).
Join the pieces with the two side panels.
End with the 'inverted square' in the centre.

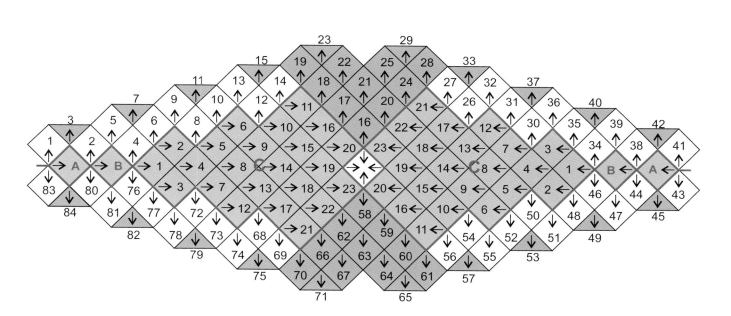

Shawl no 15

This shawl is not very large but
it sits well on your shoulders.

Intermediate

ROWAN
Pure Wool DK
Hyacinth - 026

4 balls

ROWAN
Pure Wool DK
Anthracite - 003

3 balls

ROWAN
Pure Wool DK
Black - 004

3 balls

Techniques
Knit cast on
Garter stitch
All squares are worked with decreases with distinct knit stitches

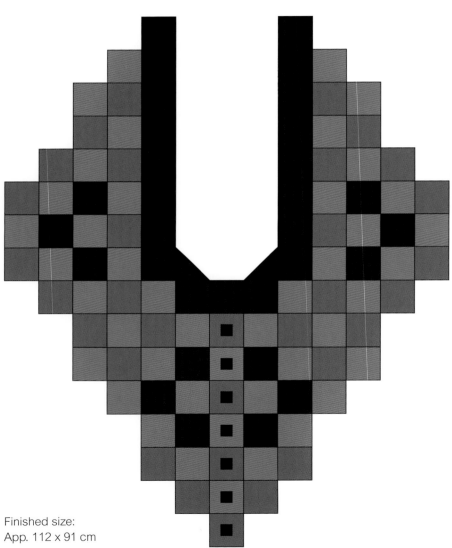

Finished size:
App. 112 x 91 cm

74

Description

Work the squares in the order shown in the chart.

Begin with the two sides and end with the stripe of 'inverted squares' down the back.

Be careful to place the corner stitch correctly, so that the diagonal knit stitches (the decreases) are flush.

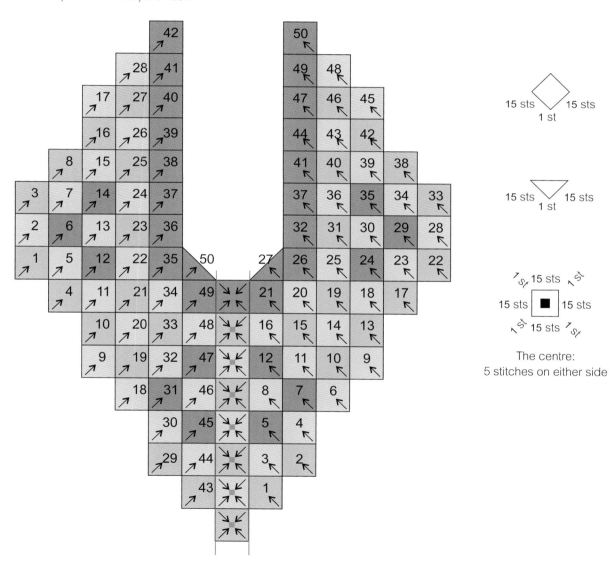

15 sts / 15 sts
1 st

15 sts / 15 sts
1 st

1 st 15 sts 1 st
15 sts ■ 15 sts
1 st 15 sts 1 st

The centre:
5 stitches on either side

Shawl no 16

It was getting late before we had finished taking the pictures, and then a warm shawl was very welcome.

Intermediate

ROWAN
Creative Focus Worsted
Copper - 02190

1 balls

ROWAN
Creative Focus Worsted
Nickel - 00401

2 balls

ROWAN
Creative Focus Worsted
Ebony - 00500

2 balls

ROWAN
Creative Focus Worsted
Natural - 00100

4 balls

Techniques
Knit cast on
Garter stitch
All squares are worked with decreases with distinct knit stitches

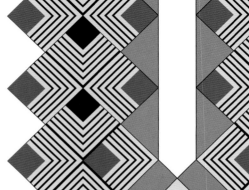

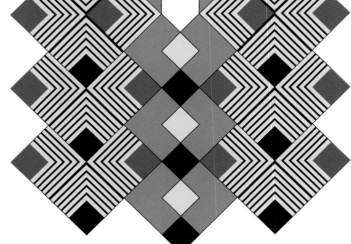

10cm/4in
10cm/4in
24 rows
20 sts

UK
7

US
7

4.5 mm

Finished size:
App. 140 x 102 cm

Description

Work the squares in the order shown in the chart.

Begin with the two sides and end with the stripe of 'inverted squares' down the back.

Be careful to place the corner stitch correctly, so that the diagonal knit stitches (the decreases) are flush.

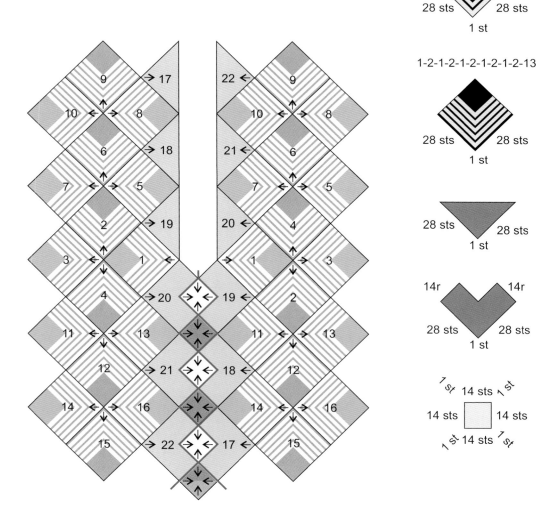

2-1-2-1-2-1-2-1-2-14

28 sts   28 sts

1 st

1-2-1-2-1-2-1-2-1-2-13

28 sts   28 sts

1 st

28 sts   28 sts

1 st

14r   14r

28 sts   28 sts

1 st

1 st   14 sts   1 st

14 sts   14 sts

1 st   14 sts   1 st

Yarn List

The following yarns were used in this book:

Rowan
Pure Wool DK

100% Super Wash Wool
Yardage: 50 grams = app. 130 meters

Rowan
Creative Focus Worsted

75 p.c. Wool, 25 p.c. Alpaca
Yardage: 100 grams = app. 200 meters

Schachenmayr
Alpaka

100 p.c. Alpaca
Yardage: 50 grams = app. 100 meters